Solidified

Solmarie Santiago

This paperback published in the United States in 2015 by CreateSpace an Amazon Company.
410 Terry Ave North
Seattle, WA 98109-5210
www.createspace.com
Published in paperback in 2015 by Create Space
Published in The United States of America in 2015
ISBN 978-1511609357
Illustration by Alain Duchateau

DEDICATION

Solidified is dedicated to Shalimar Muniz, my inspiration in so many ways and the strongest person I know. May you continue to grow and reflect on your own triumphs through the whirlwind of life.

ABOUT

Solidified is a collection of poems written through out a lifetime. Let's first head to *Californication,* a galaxy of excitability. *Solidified* then takes you to a time of true love with *Stay.* Enter a world of emotions, vulnerability and sincerity in *She is Beautiful* and *Fem.* Our quest ends with the simplicity of *The Life We Live.*

CONTENTS

Titles

Californication

I'm lost in the aftermath of a rainy day

My mind is trapped in a maze, a reality I cannot face

I gave up control in order to find my way

But now I find myself in an unknown space

I'm crying out for direction, but then I push it away

I'm stuck in the middle of my own game

Yet I'm not winning, my opponent stole my play

I fear my own intentions, my feelings are a daze

Should I give in to temptation? It's so easy to fall out of God's grace

In a flash, life was different; I lost all sense of self

My flesh is enjoying it all, while my heart is crying out for help

I grow tired in a battle between bad and good

At least in the past I have always seen where I stood

Where my future was, where my life would be

These are things today that I can no longer see

This is where I take a right turn and get on the road to redemption

I refuse to let my dreams slip through my fingers

In me lies, too much potential

I will not let myself drown in this river of liberation

If I fall or slip it will be only for one sin

Lord forgive me, for I'm on my way to Californication...

Secret

I hold your hand as these moments pass us by

If it's hard for karma to look away, I suggest she tries

Now I'm standing still in a confused state

I let you in, held you tight, was that a mistake?

I can't get you out of my head

My walls are down, my defenses are dead

But I can't help but to love this feeling

Your voice, your body, your touch, got me fieding

Destiny took a wide turn and brought us to this

Who would have thought you and me...the one I used to diss

And I was the one you used to tease

Now I'm the one who you miss

When you're not touching me, having me   I'm hard for you to resist

If you only knew you make it hard for me to breathe

But I can't let you see that much

You already know too much

I have to take a step back

Remember the past

Can I stay loyal to my wrath?

I can't help but to smile every time you call my name

The way you look at me takes me down that lane

When I'm with you everything is okay

I feel like I'm fourteen again, giggling as our numbers come together playing F.L.A.M.E

You brought me back to myself   I never felt so free

And you're sitting there not knowing what you did to me

You'll always have a spot in my heart

No matter what this turns out to be

I learned to live with the fact that   you don't even belong to me...

Underneath it All

I took a sip of your drink of passion

A taste of your love with no precaution

I looked into your soul

Dove deep into the hidden parts of you

Under all of that thick skin I found you

You who needs no introduction

You and I are true companions

A wild love impossible to tame

You intrigue me with your words

You astound me with your actions

Your sincerity is what keeps me here

Seeing this hidden realm within your being makes it clear

You have turned into my perfect man

Can you please not ever disappear?

Poison

You are toxic

Like sweet marmalade that turns sour as soon as you dare to taste it

You are vile

Evil hidden behind a fountain of diamonds and rivers of satisfaction

You are poison

A pure look of beauty and innocence evolves into a force of anger and hate

Have you ever heard rage in silence?

Have you ever-feared words as loud as sirens?

Have you ever felt pain slowly pierce your spirit like a virus?

You are toxic

I swear to not ever forget, the darkness you help set

Mine

Serenade me with your song

Infect me with your lies

Tell me what I want to hear

Ignore my foolish cry

Your light breaks through the dark skies

My heart breaks with the sound of goodbye

Tomorrow is another day when we can give it a second try

Life is a labyrinth watch out for the walls that arise

If you take me back for just one night

I'll make sure my perfume reminisces in your loveless spite

This story's ending my soul will write

You and I always until the end of time

My Prince Charming

Your memories linger in the heavy air

The face of the one who had my soul at first glare

You broke my heart plenty of times

For some reason I can't forget you as much as I try

I remember your touch as if you were here

But destiny played a trick on us; you're nowhere near

The last time I saw you it was clear

The bright shiny dagger still reflects my tears

You hurt me so many times that I have lost count

How do you still have me tied up and bound?

The man who nobody will understand

My prince charming, my right hand

Now we live our separate lives   our new routines aligned
with theirs

Our new futures with them we stand

We look in their eyes with sincerity

When they look back into ours, can they find eternity?

For me you will remain my secret ending

You're forever in my heart

My unfinished puzzle

My prince charming, you are trouble

Stay

Feelings soar faster than light

Rapidly falling prisoner to your eyes

You broke the chains protecting my heart

Am I safe?   Or will you tear me apart?

My world changed all at once

You came into my life and already made a mark

Drew a map all the way to my heart

I hope you never have to find your way back

Sleeping Pills

Pills hide under my pillow each night

They help mend the guilt I feel inside

As I lay next to him in this empty spread

While what I want is asleep in another bed

How do I tell him that I'm wasting his time?

That the love I seek is another kind

Restlessness changing me and I have changed my mind

Forget our plans and leave our memories behind

He's not home yet I must take them now

I enter that solemn realm of peace where vulnerability is allowed

Where I can sit with the gods of a misunderstood comprehension

See things beyond our reality and fly far passed our inception

Realize that this is only a moment in a complicated spectrum

As I lay me down to sleep I take this pill and submerge into a judgment free reflection

The Cheating Wife

Blame it on the cheating wife

But no one sees her tears at night

When he puts her down and makes her cry

He rolls over and falls asleep

Snoring past her sleepless dreams

Too prideful to notice how far he has gone

But when she cheats it's all her fault

To make him mad it doesn't take much

She's trying to talk but he doesn't budge

He doesn't see he's in the wrong

But when she cheats it's all her fault

The Dotted Line

The shine in my eyes faded more each day

The love I once felt slowly slipped away

Prayed to God every night for our recovery

But God refused to help with my discovery

You were the perfect guy, a Martini with just the right amount of vermouth

But when perfection fades you're left with just the truth

We let each other down and couldn't salvage this

Guess our next move is to finally let go of this

Life will bring us new stories to write

The spirit of our past will always rest by our sides

Remember the late night walks around Union Square?

The way you used to kiss me in the crowded subway without a care?

We couldn't live without each other on Friday nights

We were crazy about one another, carved our names on the tree of life

Somehow forever disappeared and we grew weary of each other's time

Our flaws came to the light and we became unapologetic of our lies

The time has arrived hold me tight on this last night

In the morning we face the rest of our entire lives

Just sign your name on the dotted line and your divorced will be finalized

Waterfalls

Life flows like a fierce waterfall

Sirens sing the song of a relentless downfall

What if you had taken a different route?

Your fate would have been written mercifully without a doubt

This is your path so take it now

Will you take it with your head held high and proud?

Or dwell on the mistakes that keep you bound?

The key to your prison cell was in your back pocket all along

You were just too busy watching others break their own falls

Learning for yourself is the secret behind triumph

Consume your demons with your newfound fire

Life flows like a waterfall loud and strong

Swim through the valley of doubt and drown those tendencies that kept you on the ground

Flourish…for your time is now

To no man

I watch her as she laughs and plays

The innocence of a child was harshly taken away

Shhh...She's quiet as she drowns her tears

Her dark secret being revealed is her biggest fear

She pretends to be happy...she's a normal girl

Her beauty is undeniable...she's a perfect pearl

The nightmare she lives is indescribable

God just seems to be a fairytale in a book called The Bible

Nobody can stop this monster from killing her inside

Time after time she endures the pain of this tough life

She thinks the silence is worth it

She wants her little brothers to smile

His twisted words telling her not to worry...it's all-worthwhile

The hate corrupts her young heart as evil tears her apart

Only the walls that surround her can explain her broken heart

She was once an angel but her wings were cut

She tumbled all the way down to a Hell that was all too dark

One day the truth will be told she tells herself

But who will put me back together?

Who will pick up the pieces?

Who is my defender?

She knows one thing for sure; to no man she will ever surrender

She is beautiful

I saw her as soon as I ran to the first seat on the subway

It was unbelievable how every time I sneaked a glance at her she looked even more stunning

Her eyes wide and bright

Lips luscious and perfectly dipped in Mac

She wore a fur coat that made her look like a superstar

Her brows stopped perfectly before the end of her cat eye

She steadily looked out the window watching the motion of the dirty dark walls pass her by

But she wasn't there...

Her thoughts made her prisoner of another world

She would occasionally smirk at the outcome of the future she daydreamed about

She glanced over at me once or twice

But each time I made sure to look concentrated on the ad about Spanish rice

Where is she going?

What does she think about right before she falls asleep?

Who has hurt her?

What Novela makes her weep?

Her purpose today was to impact my life

I left my small world and tried to decipher her strive

She will never know what she did for me

I am now selfless and our connection is irrefutable

She will be blind to this but she is still beautiful

Rain

The grey sky filled his soul with wonder

Each raindrop broke through the clouds like a speeding bullet

His glasses filled with tiny little drops of water and his blonde hair fell heavy on his head now

The cold air cooled his rage and the rain cleansed his aching thoughts

With every breath he took he felt his reality becoming true

Feeling misled and lost was a feeling he knew all too well

Where will life take me? What should I do next?

Sometimes he sat alone in the harbor watching the water move in small waves

Nature was at times his only friend

Walking home today was different

Although he was soaked he felt free

He finally arrived at home and inserted his key into the wooden door to his mother's brownstone

Surprise! A crowd inside yelled

Astonished to see his family united in his single mom's home he looked up at the banner above that read, "We Know"

This day filled his soul with certainty that the world just budged a little bit

"We love you son" dad said, as he hugged a new man, a happy gay man.

Fem

Wear your crown o fearless one for the reign is yours

Stand tall to your adversaries and watch as they all fall

Delicate as a rose petal yet strong as an ox

Just look at her essence, she must be a god

The way her spirit roars in the calming melody of her song

So beautiful, so stunning, there's no doubt she has it all

No man can come close to the strength of a woman's soul

Soaring through life with such grace and adamant control

A powerful being given much to handle and the knowledge to never fail

You are perfectly put together, always sturdy and never frail

Don't be ashamed to dry your tears as emotions feed our core

Her intuition a secret weapon in the most frightening of storms

The power that you hold is undeniable

Sensuality that can make an entire empire crumble

So lift your chin and fix your posture

You have a world to take over and a destiny ahead sure to prosper

Wear your crown o fearless one for the reign you have conquered

New York City Summers

It's like summers in New York

Exciting and new

Expect nothing less than something curiously true

So hot you want to take it off

But so right that it can never be wrong

New places, new faces, he must be new

He wears a smile on his face, jeans J. Crew

He's probably just a tourist headed for Time Square

Bumping into New Yorkers, checking into Foursquare

Let's hang out at Verlaine and maybe later the West Village

Maybe we will run into Jay Z or even Calvin Harris

That reminds me, are we going to Shake Shack later?

Maybe we will have a New York night hang out with a random waiter

Party at Hudson Terrace and end up at the diner on 13th

Brunch at Sons of Essex and day drinking at Bourbon Street

Where will we wake up? Who knows?

It's like summers in New York

Let's go where the wind blows

The Life We Live

We evoked victory and watched our insecurities go

Our soaring spirits march tall through the bumpy road

These struggles will scar our hearts, but can never stomp our art

We will keep walking through the rain

Love and strength pumping through our veins

Every emotion we will embrace

Wake up a warrior each living day

Who are we if not the tasks we face?

The wind is cold and the streets are dark

But we refuse to let our hopes drop

We will keep running at the speed of light

Boots in the mud but heads held high

This life is a beautiful journey full of sin

I promise to make it all worth it before I see him

I pray you forgive our little tricks

Cheers to the turbulence and this life we live

About the Author

Solmarie Santiago was born in Arecibo, Puerto Rico. Her family moved to Rochester, New York when she was 7-years old. Writing has served as her way of complete expression since she could remember. She has been writing stories, poems and songs since she was a little girl.

Solmarie is also a celebrity news blogger keeping the world updated on all-things Hollywood on www.thesolciety.com and through various other online publications.

"When you take on the title of a writer you give destiny the okay to allow you to live experiences that other people do not. How else could you find the material to intrigue those who read your wacky tales?"

Made in the USA
Las Vegas, NV
29 February 2024